Fly Not Yet, My Princess

A Prayer Answered

CARISSA A. ULRICH

Illustrated by V.A.U.

ISBN 1-57502-157-9

Second Printing 1999

Printed in the USA by

Morris Publishing
3212 E Hwy 30
Kearney, NE 68847
800-650-7888

I dedicate this book to:

God, for his miracles;

My loving husband, Todd, and our two wonderful daughters, who are my constant source of joy;

Gerald, Jan, Brad, Aaron, Marlene, Tad, and Stacy for their never-ending love and support;

Michelle, my honest critic and true friend;

Lynn, who believed in me long before I did;

Tracy, for her typesetting;

And everyone else who has touched my life, whether quietly or with the blasting sound of trumpets. It is your support that has given me the courage to realize my dream.

Preface

On January 14, 1994, one of the most bitterly cold days of the year, I gave birth to our second daughter. She was our ray of sunshine on that bleak winter day. What should have been simply spectacular, however, was nothing close to simple. The spectacular part quickly vanished also, when I began to hemorrhage profusely soon after delivery. I was then separated from my newborn daughter. I underwent not one, but two grueling surgeries that evening and found myself fighting for my life. I was transferred to an intensive care unit in a neighboring city the next morning due to my critical condition. I became enclosed in a world of pain: blood transfusions, blood clots, cramping, burning, needles and more needles. It seemed to be suffocating me. My life was a barrage of emotions, pain, and fear.

After finally being discharged to home, I was admitted to yet another hospital eight weeks later with more complications. I went through more testing, more pain, more separation from my family. In the year and a half following, I suffered from chronic abdominal and back pain, nightmares, and emotional anguish. At the young age of twenty-seven, a hysterectomy followed and I spent more time in recovery -- both physically and emotionally. My life had been forever changed.

In the midst of all the negativity, I found myself clinging to every glimmer of hope I could find. God had blessed me with another beautiful, healthy daughter. She was a gem! God had also given me a second chance to live -- to love, to laugh, and to join with my husband in watching our children grow. It was by shaking hands with death that I was introduced to true life for the very first time. It was an awakening of sorts. It was my miracle.

I am grateful that I am surrounded by strong, supportive people. My husband and children, my friends and family members gave me the strength and courage to move past my pain. With their help, I was able to find the peace in my heart that had remained hidden for almost two years. They helped me find my way back.

In the midst of my loved ones, stood one very strong man. He was a man who went into a hospital utility closet to pray for a miracle ... a man who had enough faith for both of us ... a man who prayed for me when I could not pray for myself ... a man I proudly call Dad ..... my father.

INTRICATE
FAMILY
WeAVe

Age 6

Chapter 1

Intricate Family Weave

There once was a father who went to visit his daughter in the hospital. She had just delivered a 7 lb. 13 oz. baby girl. It was so exciting to have another grandchild! However, things did not progress smoothly with his daughter. She had begun to hemorrhage profusely and her life was at stake. He watched his daughter as she lie there crying -- begging the nurses to stop her pain. As her blood pressure continued to drop, her pulse rate escalated. They had to get her into the operating room. There was no time to waste.

As they wheeled her down the hallway on the cart, he walked beside her. Before they took her into the operating room, he leaned down to hug and kiss her. His teardrops fell onto her face, mixing with her own tears and sliding down her cheeks.

"I love you, Princess," he whispered.

"I know," she said, "I love you, too."

The father then walked down the hallway to a utility closet. He went inside and shut the door to the world outside. He spent a great deal of time in there, leaving others only to wonder what he could possibly be doing. His wife worried about him, as well as her daughter.

This man longed for peace, silence, and a solitude in which to pray. His hands were tightly grasped together, his knuckles ashen. This middle-aged man turned suddenly old -- his whole body trembled.

So much had happened in the past few hours. It seemed too horrible to be real. He thought of his little girl, his princess. He had always protected her. How could he protect her now? This devastating turn of events threatened to steal his daughter from him, and the world as he knew it would never be the same. As he listened to the faint cries of his daughter's newborn baby, he knew the only protection he had left to give her was prayer.

So he prayed.
He prayed with his heart.
He prayed with his mind.
He prayed with his soul.
He prayed for the one thing
that could save his daughter.
He prayed for a miracle.

Fly Not Yet, My Princess
A father's prayer

Fly not yet, my princess
We will not say good-bye
Your newborn needs her mommy
We can not watch you die

The birth of your child was complicated
We fear your life may end --
I pray to heaven for healing
With a miracle, you will mend

That look of panic on your face
And then the loss of blood
All your loved ones crying
A huge emotional flood

Your mom and I are racked with pain
Your husband paces the floor
Your four-year-old holds her baby sister
Whom an hour ago you bore

As I pray for you
I look to the sky
Must God really take my princess?
The thought now makes me cry

I pray my princess won't fly just yet
Please hear my cries, dear Lord
She is our angel here on earth
Her death, we can't afford

Fly not yet, my princess
You've so much left to do
We need our sister, wife, and friend
Our daughter, now the mother of two

. . . . I've witnessed a miracle from on high
The Lord carried you through the night
I watched you wake, dear princess,
To view the morning light

You will not fly yet, Princess
Heaven will wait for you
You will remain our angel on earth
For you still have much to do

To You: Gerald Hall

5

Father

F   is for feelings he hides a bit

A   is for amusing, very sharp wit

T   is for teacher of right versus wrong

H   is for heartstrings a mile long

E   is for expert in finding the good
in the bad

R   is for revered -- a terrific dad

My Mother, My Friend

You nurtured me as a child
And you never stopped giving
There were always hugs and kisses
You added love to living

You protected me -- kept me safe
From the monsters of the night
And when I was ill with fever
You rocked me and held me tight

Your face was always in the crowd
At every school event
You were always in my corner, Mom
Do you know how much that meant?

You instilled in me good values
You and Dad taught me to pray
Through my faith, I could find the sun
On the gloomiest of days

You led me into this world years ago
I was your pride and joy -- no doubt
And when death knocked upon my door
You were not ready to lead me out

You squeezed my hand tightly
Whispering, "Don't give up the fight!"
And holding on to your courage
I made it through the night

Who has given me more than you?
Always my friend -- my mother
I can not think of anyone
To me, there is no other

To You: Janet Hall

Treasure Every Minute

I remember arriving home with you
My bundle, so fragile and small
Now you're a toddler with a handful of crayons
Your artwork covers our wall

It seems like only yesterday
I bounced you on my knee
Now already you're ten years old
Tell me, how can this be?

Junior high -- your very first day
I am more nervous than you
Wasn't fourth grade just yesterday?
Somewhere I blinked and you grew

It wasn't all that long ago
You entered seventh grade
Graduation is now upon us
Oh ... the memories that we've made

Last time you received a diploma
You graduated senior high
Now you've completed college
As a tear escapes my eye

The music sings of memories
As your wedding guests are seated
I tried to slow time as you grew older
I see I was defeated

A familiar sound from years gone by
Now your sweet newborn baby cries
Treasure every moment, my child
When you're living life, time flies!

Grandpa

G is for generous in every way

R is for reminiscing about yesterday

A is for adventurous mind of a child

N is for narrator of stories so wild

D is for devoted to family ties

P is for practical and wise

A is for ageless in his grandchildren's eyes

Grandma

G   is for giving of herself and her time

R   is for reading nursery rhymes

A   is for appreciating the littlest things

N   is for nurturing, yet allowing you wings

D   is for defending unconditionally

M   is for maintaining harmony

A   is for adoring her family

To You: Christine Hall

Husband

H   is for helpmate in life

U   is for unity with his wife

S   is for strong soul and mind

B   is for big-hearted and kind

A   is for appeaser when he needs to be

N   is for naturally fun-loving and free

D   is for dreams he makes a reality

Wife

W   is for warmhearted and kind

I   is for intelligent mind

F   is for forever sharing

E   is for endlessly caring

Son

S   is for scurrying, on the run

O   is for one big bundle of fun

N   is for naturally bright as the sun

Daughter

D   is for darling, little girl so sweet

A   is for active pitter-patter of feet

U   is for uplifting kisses and hugs

G   is for gum she hides under the rugs

H   is for honest, so innocent and fair

T   is for tangles she gets in her hair

E   is for excitement twinkling in her eye

R   is for rare gem -- money can't buy

To You: My Precious Daughters

Mother

M   is for miraculous giver of life

O   is for oasis in the desert of strife

T   is for tears she helps to wipe dry

H   is for handmade quilts that she ties

E   is for echoes she leaves in your mind

R   is for role model -- the ultimate kind

Bountiful Gifts

You give of yourself
And through the years I've learned,
That in exchange for your help
You ask nothing in return

Your advice flows freely from your heart
I'm assured you really care
And when my pain tips the scale,
I count on you to be there

Your soul mate in life was lost to you
Devastated, you stood alone
Nurturing your sons as seeds --
Beautifully they have been sewn

Thank you for your love,
Your guidance and concern
You've earned your wisdom through living --
From you, we all can learn

To You: Marlene Ulrich

After Thirty Years Of Marriage

Grandchildren think punch bowls
        make good fish bowls
Your towels are in shreds
You're more than a bit embarrassed
By the sheets upon your beds

Your slicer doesn't slice
Your toaster doesn't toast
Your pots burn your rice
Your roaster doesn't roast

Your serving bowls have served their time
Your crock pot went to pot
But think of throwing things away?
Absolutely not!

Wee Feet

There is something about those tiny feet
That makes us love them so
It won't be but a blink of an eye
Before those little feet grow

When first they learn to toddle,
They wander onto the grass
All ten toes scrunch right up
Upon the fertile mass

Baby's toes live to breathe,
Out in the open air.
Socks are quite a hindrance
And shoes -- too much to bear!

Wee feet encounter wet and mushy
While in pursuit of the garden hose.
Mud feels soft and cushy
When squished between those tiny toes

Baby's feet are for kissing,
Pink as petals and chubby, too.
Always exploring and on the run
Seldom resting, "Oh, this is true!"

Have Courage, My Child

The courage to love
        the image in the mirror
The courage to listen
        when you don't want to hear --
The courage to laugh
        in the midst of your pain
The courage to dance
        in the down-pouring rain --
The courage to extend your hand
        to a lost soul in need
The courage to abandon the caboose
        and dare to lead --
The courage to live each day
        as if it's your last
The courage to forgive
        mistakes of the past

Brother

B   is for boy who enjoys the outdoors

R   is for radiant smile that soars

O   is for often times rough and tumble

T   is for terrific, yet ever humble

H   is for handyman; he's the best

E   is for energized, full of zest

R   is for registered sister's pest

Sister

S   is for safety net; she's always there

I   is for ingenuity, that which is rare

S   is for straightforward, a bit too bold

T   is for theatrics; she continually unfolds

E   is for effervescent like the ocean tide

R   is for real friend in which you confide

My Best Friend

You admired me at my best
You didn't fold when sadness pressed
You continued to love me at my worst
You quenched my emotional thirst
You held my hand when I couldn't squeeze back
You hugged me while death threatened and attacked
You never ignored or dismissed my cries
You tenderly wiped the tears from my eyes
You woke me from nightmares to say, "It's not real."
When I began to crumble, my pain you would steal
You listened so long -- you almost forgot how to speak
You carried me when I was weak
You never gave up, never quit
Through all the turmoil, you kept your wit
You made me laugh in the midst of my pain
When fear attacked my existence, you kept me sane
You prayed for me both day and night
You never let me give up the fight
You were more than my husband; you were my best friend
You loved me completely and you helped me to mend
You are an extraordinary, beautiful part of my life
Thank you for carrying me through my strife

To You: Todd

20

Chapter 2

Cascade Of Inspiration

Loss -- we are all faced with it in one form or another during our lifetime: the loss of a job, the loss of time, the loss of control, financial loss, and the loss of a loved one. What can we gain from loss?

For nine months, I had anticipated the birth of my second child and the hours and days that would follow: the joy, the excitement, the bonding between mother and child, the gleam in my daughter's eyes while looking at her new baby brother or sister.

Being separated from my newborn daughter after her birth was a huge sense of loss for me. My newborn remained in one hospital, while I was transferred to another hospital. I was unable to leisurely hold her and absorb her newness -- her innocence. I was unable to nurse her, to bond with her. The oneness we had shared for nine months was suddenly gone.

The sadness I felt was immeasurable when my husband brought our baby home ... and I remained hospitalized. I knew my daughter would never again be two days old or five days old. Time was slipping away from me.

When my husband first brought our children to visit me, I was too weak to even hold our baby. He held her close to my face so I could at least look at her. I was her mother, and it was as if we were being introduced to one another. I wasn't physically able to hold my four-year-old. I wasn't able to nurse my baby. I could not embrace my husband. After my family went home that evening, I began to cry. The sense of loss and sadness I was feeling began to consume me.

At my weakest point, God raised my heavy, swollen eyelids to see the picture that lay on the table beside me. It was a Polaroid of my husband and our two daughters that had been taken just the day before. The picture was my four-year-old daughter's gift to me -- a gift of renewal.

In that moment, I realized that I wasn't alone in my pain. They, too, were suffering. I also realized that my family would always be with me, and I with them. The fact that I couldn't physically hold them didn't matter. Because, you see, I had been holding my family all along -- in my heart. And they, too, held me. And no amount of pain or suffering would be able to shatter the embracing of our hearts.

In the midst of my sense of loss, I had gained a new understanding. It was an understanding that would give me the strength to carry on. I now knew the true meaning of family, love, motherhood, and "for better or for worse". Through my sense of loss, I gained. The inspiration I found in that moment was truly breathtaking.

Prayer

Precious moments spent with God

Requests and thank-yous from the heart

Angels listening to our wails and whispers

Yearning for the answers we desire

Eager to speak with our Creator --

Revelations abound

Hope

Having confidence in the

One who is our

Precious source of

Everything good

Faith

Following the Lord

And believing

In life everlasting,

Trusting that

Heaven awaits

Please Grant Me

God, please grant me serenity
In this world of hurry
Where fast forward is the only speed
Progression with fastest fury

God, please grant me peace
To fill my heart and mind
When my soul is tangled up in knots
Unravel it -- unwind

God, please grant me faith
Innocence, like that of a child
Help me to believe in myself
Yet keep my ego mild

God, please grant me love
As profound as the deepest sea
Easily given to my friends
Likewise, my enemies

God, please grant me strength
Wisdom and understanding
Help me to be forgiving
Accepting, not demanding

Help Me To Sleep

Please help me to sleep
When fear grips me
Worry overtakes me
Doubt questions me
And sadness weakens me

Please help me to sleep
When burdened by guilt
When anger boils over
When depression is my closest friend
And when the hurt stabs like a knife

But most importantly, Lord
Remind me to count my blessings instead of sheep
And please watch over me as I sleep

Call On Jesus

My dearest Jesus, I call on You
My life is in shambles -- What shall I do?
I need your guidance and your love
Look down upon me with grace from heaven above
My dearest Jesus, please cleanse my soul
Make my heart right and help me to be whole
Take my hand gently -- show me the way
And be my guide until the judgment day
My dearest Jesus, You died for me
And rose again -- from sin, You set me free
I thank You, Jesus, and I will be
As true to You, as You have been to me

Trust

To believe you can

Rely on Him --

Understanding that He

Suffered death on the cross

To save us from our own sin

Laughter

Laughter is a gift from God
An amazing thing -- laughter
It heals wounds
And softens even the hardest hearts

Laughter can make fantasies seem real
And reality becomes a little less scary
Amidst the sound of giggles --
Hearts dance to the sound of kind laughter

Laughter will save you from tears
Or drive you toward them
Laughter is a precious gift --
Free medicine that heals

When An Angel Whispers, Listen

Hear ye! Hear ye! An angel whispers
Fall upon the sound
Lend your ear
Hang upon every utterance

When an angel whispers, listen
Listen with intent -- strain to hear
Listen, not just with ears
Listen with heart, mind and soul

When angelic words are whispered
Be all ears
Entrap the underlying meaning
Embrace it

Lend not a deaf ear
Then, too, your eyes will be enlightened
Listen --
And you will no doubt see

The Greatest Gift

His eyes must have told the story,
Upon his head, a crown of thorns.
The thorns dug ever so deep,
Soon his flesh was ragged and torn.

The blood trickled and dripped,
And made pools in the hot sand below.
To become etched in time throughout eternity
And forever in our minds.

Then came darkness --
Turbulence shook the land.
The screams of believers pierced the air
Like the nails pierced Jesus' hands.

Humiliated and forsaken,
He did not curse the pain.
He endured the pain that was meant to be ours.
He did not die in vain.

He took our sins upon himself.
He died so we could live.
The greatest gift we could receive,
Jesus then did give.

My Wish For You

My wish for you is love abounding
As far as the eye can see
My wish for you is pride
In being the person you are meant to be

My wish for you is sunshine
Helping to brighten your day
My wish for you is laughter
To wash your tears away

My wish for you is friendships
You'll cherish throughout your life
My wish for you is God's loving grace
To help you conquer strife

My wish for you is joy
From deep within your heart
My wish for you is a loving family
Of which you can be a part

My wish for you is contentment
In whatever you choose to do
My wish for you is the remembrance
That Jesus will always be a friend to you

The Star's Message

I walk the long distance
Gazing up at the stars
Looking at the highway
Watching all the cars

Rush - Zoom - Flash!
The cars race past
While one heavenly star in the sky
Lingers ... its brilliance cast

People are like cars
Living much too fast
They've forgotten to enjoy
Numerous days passed

The star is of God
Speaking in a way
Giving us the chance to change
The way we live today

Twinkling God's message
Slow down the pace
Constantly racing toward tomorrow
Leaves us with yesterdays

Wicked Chameleon

Wickedness is not always present
In full manner -- sprouting horns
It may not display a pitchfork
And bleeding crimson cape --
Exhibiting serene innocence
The devil's grin may hide
Adorned in flowers so lush
The danger sign fades from view --
It may not reek of garbage
Yet the mind is twisted up in knots
Packaged in paper so brilliant
Beautifully gift-wrapped is the wicked core --
Wickedness may dress in a three piece suit
Just the same as homeless rags
The true master of deception
With a mask for every occasion --
Beware of the chameleon ...
Just because you can not see it
Doesn't mean it isn't there!

Spiritual Ride

Let us go on a spiritual ride
A man named Jesus will be our guide
The Kingdom is our destiny
Living for Christ, we have the key
There is no charge, no toll, no fee
Entrance is through the Almighty

There you will find no pain -- no crime
No need for keeping track of time
No turmoil -- no one is ill
You don't check-out; there is no bill
In this Kingdom, there is no fear
No sadness causing salty tears
Let us go on a spiritual ride
A man named Jesus will be our guide
Trust him to bring you to the gate
Heaven is where true life awaits

Risks

To smile at another
Not knowing if a smile will be returned,
To direct your ship
Into waters uncharted,
To love completely
Fearing rejection,
To forgive
And trust once again,
To open the door to your heart
Letting another enter,
To face new challenges
Without backing down,
To believe in God wholeheartedly
Whom you have never seen,
This is to risk --

To never risk
Is the greatest risk of all!

True Victory

Life has its problems
That you must face
A handful of wrongs
That you want to erase
There are decisions to make
And options to choose
You aspire to win
Yet fear you will lose --
Start with faith
In God, you can trust
Add daily prayer
It's a definite must --
When confusion is knocking on your door
And trouble lurks too close
Rely on God, for He's the one
Who will chase away those ghosts --
To win, there need not be an opponent
Not even a real contest ...
True victory comes
When your soul is at its best
And in the midst of turmoil
Your heart can find rest

A Sinner's Prayer

In the quiet night
My heart pounds ever so loudly
I view my past before me
Not everything is looked upon proudly

My faults have been many
Myself I can not forgive
My guilty conscience plays on my errors
My mistakes, I continue to relive

On this quiet night
I look up to the skies
I pray, dear Lord
That You will hear my cries

Please forgive me and help me to forget
The troubles of my heart
Let tomorrow's morning sun
Bring for me, a brand new start

A Vision Of Heaven

The end is near,
Or is it just the beginning?
The cool breeze blows through the trees
And the leaves begin to fall
The stream flows briskly
Joining hands with the raging river

The clouds are ever so fluffy
Piled high -- one upon the other
The birds soar overhead
Lifting their wings to the breeze
BEAUTY -- such beauty
Angels appear on the other side of the river --
No words are spoken
As they motion for me to cross
The sun's ray, as if commanded,
Has now escaped the clouds
Becoming a golden path upon the water
Without hesitation, I cross the water
As if it were natural ground
I approach the other side
Only to look back and see the massive crowd:
Jumping into the water,
Falling, drowning,
Begging to be rescued --
I step upon the shore
Enthralled by the mighty Kingdom
Their silence is broken
As the angels speak these words,
"Few will follow.
Few will enter.
Welcome and God bless. "
Suddenly I awoke
Only to enter this earthly world again
There is excruciating pain and sadness ...
I'm told my time is dwindling
I close my eyes and wait --
But I fear not
For my vision spoke of incredible peace,
Of a not so far away Kingdom,
My eternal Home

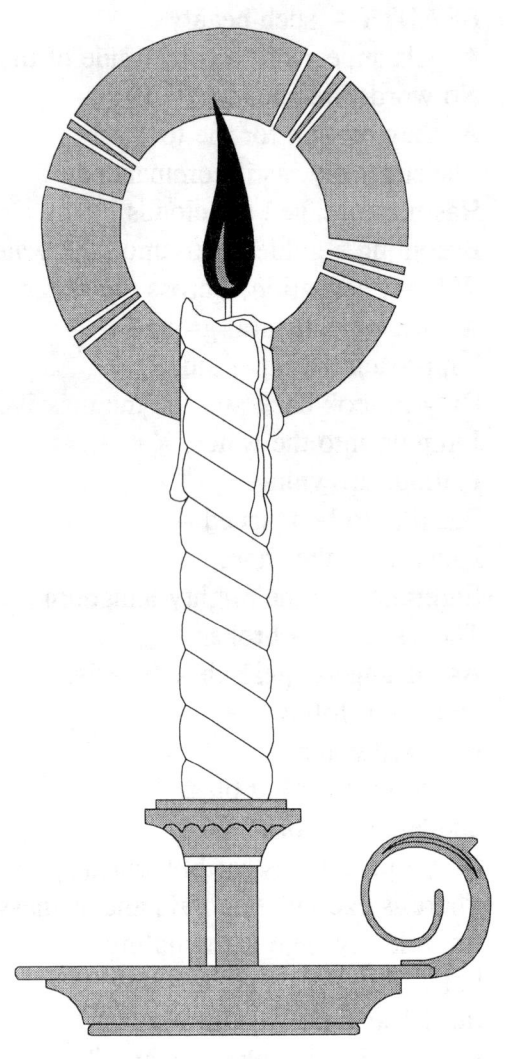

Chapter 3

A Flicker In The Dark

TIME -- too quick, too slow, never enough, too much. Is it ever the right TIME?

It is odd how TIME seems to stand still in the midst of pain. In the hours between 8:00 pm on January 14th and 7:00 am January 15th, I lived, what seemed to me, a lifetime. Seconds ticked by ever so slowly, forming one long minute after another. Those eleven hours seemed to expand far beyond my previous twenty-five years. I remember waking on Saturday morning thinking I had been hospitalized for weeks. At that time, it had been only one day.

Given eleven hours on any other day, and I would be complaining that I didn't have enough TIME to accomplish what needed doing. I mean, after all, eleven hours isn't even half a day!

Our conception of TIME is so relative. Is there really such a thing as standard TIME?

In TIME, I slowly began to heal and my pain eventually subsided. Yet I wonder what a struggle life must be for those who are in constant pain -- constant emotional upheaval.

What is TIME like for those who don't have supportive friends or family ... for those without faith ... for those who enter darkness one day and never find their way out? In their world of long drawn-out TIME, who or what is the light in their darkness? There are those who seem to have it all: a loving family, a good job, a great spiritual connection. Yet they still view TIME as their enemy.

I have come to realize that even a small flashlight in a world of complete darkness can be like a beacon in the night to a searching soul.

Each one of us has the power to act as a light in the dark world of a sad heart -- the littlest beam of cheer, the smallest ray of kindness, a flicker of understanding.

We may not be the cure, but we can make a difference if we take the TIME.

TIME

What TIME is it?
Do you have the correct TIME?
There is no TIME for that!
If I only had TIME

I'm just wasting TIME
Passing the TIME
Watching the clock
Waiting for the right TIME

How much TIME do you have?
What TIME can I count on you?
It's TIME to leave
I am running out of TIME

Past, present, future
Where has the TIME gone?
Tick-tock, cuckoo clock
How much TIME do I have left?

A Town Misses A Child

Folks lie awake at night
Wondering where she is
Wondering if she is breathing
Wondering if she lives

Is this child near her house?
Or is she out of state?
The community feels so helpless
As they search, ponder -- wait

They ask themselves, "What happened?
What more could have been done?"
They have so many questions
For answers, they have none

They pray to heaven above
That God will keep her in his care
The disappearance of this child
Has been too much to bear

They search each and every playground
Each small child's face
They comb each wooded area
Just looking for a trace

If only they could see her laugh
And watch her out at play
If only she would come home safely
That is what they pray

Dedicated To: Missing children
everywhere

43

A Good Tired

There's something about a "good tired"
That brings you peace inside
Your weary bones are aching
Yet your heart is full of pride

You had your scattered lists
Laying about for weeks
"I'll get to it tomorrow," you'd say,
While ambitions remained weak.

The domino effect then strikes you
One finished chore leads to the next
The neighbors see you mow the lawn
"Good Lord, she must be hexed!"

The yard is trimmed and groomed
Each room in the house beyond clean
You dump those clothes into the washer
They look and smell quite mean!

You jump into the shower
Steam rising above your head
Your sore muscles start to loosen
As you dream of lying in bed

You've one thing to do before resting
Place clean sheets upon your bed
You then enjoy the "good tired"
As you rest your weary head

Warfare Termination

Perfect silence
Worldly peace
Hush -- go to sleep
Fighting has ceased

Quiet moments
Hearts soothed -- calm
Bonded harmony
Gentle breezes carrying the Psalms

Utter contentment
Stillness towers
Lull in the storm
Repose is ours

The Color Fight

There are so many lines being drawn --
Separating
Dividing
Shattering and destroying

Positive - Negative
Day - Night
Hot - Cold
BLACK - WHITE

What is the reason?
Why must this be?
Don't look at my color --
Look inside of me

We divide ourselves by color
And stand at a defense
While all the while we cry for unity
Our division makes no sense

Whether we are black
Or whether we are white
God knows no prejudice
We are equal in his sight

Many harbor anger
At the unity of black and white
I pray I will see the day
When we will end this color fight

This Old Woman's Basket

My basket has a hole in it
But it will have to do
While others easily fill their baskets full
Some of my treasures slip right through

My basket's handle is broken
Others carry their baskets with ease
I have to lift mine from the bottom
It's a strain upon these knees

My basket is of faded color
The weaving -- short of tight
Ooh ... but the things my basket once held
Please my dreams at night

"Throw that old thing out," they say.
They just don't understand
This basket is a part of my heart
Like the dirt is of the land

My basket is an heirloom
Passed from family to family
Granted -- it doesn't hold much today
Yet it still holds memories

Why?

Why are compliments whispered
And insults shouted?
Why is fiction believed
And truth doubted?

Why are minds narrow
And tongues wide?
Why does chaos boldly live
While tranquility quietly dies?

Why does gossip take flight
Over all other news?
Why do criminals win
While victims lose?

Why does bad seem common
And good seem rare?
For the innocent
Life can be short of fair

What separates positive from negative?
Just four tiny letters ...
Let's concentrate on the positive
Hence, the world will be better

Is There A Difference?

WEBSTER says Elamite.
You say language.
Felodese or suicide,
Which is it?
It is musty.
No, it is frowsy.
Call a hackie.
Call a cabdriver.
Page five hundred forty-four,
Definition number four ---
Guy means ridicule.
What's the score?
Shall we perform a juba,
Or shall we dance?
Don't step out of your mete
And I won't cross my boundary.
Persons means people.
To purchase is to buy.
So why is there so much difference
Between you and I?

A Name

A name, a name
What is a name?
Born to the sound of gunshots
Echoing throughout the valley
Geraldine, a warrior maid --

49

A little human being
Adopted by a childless woman
Janet, a gift from God --
The first born of the queen
Full of beauty and grace
The princess, Sarah --
A child so precious
Asleep upon her mother's breast
Amanda, lovable Amanda --
Full of energy and innocence
A dimple on her chin
Ever youthful, Julia --
Born on a cool, crisp night
A fall evening, never to be forgotten
Teresa, of the harvest --
A name, a name
What is a name?

Warm Fuzzies

The world is full of unkind words and deeds
Give warm fuzzies and you plant kind seeds
Share a hug or a great big smile
One kind word can travel miles
Heartfelt compliments mean so much
A handmade gift is an added touch
Being a friend to someone in need
Is top-notch in the warm fuzzy creed
True warm fuzzies have a special way
Of adding sunshine to a gloomy day

To You: Kay Sabin

Inner Reflective Moment

We all have one in our journey through life
Sometimes planned, most often not --
A minute that attacks our very existence
Our souls start searching
Our minds play back memories
Of our time already spent

We all have that moment of inner reflection
What is truly significant?
Of absolute importance?
It's the moment to ask the tough questions
The moment to ponder their answers
We focus on our journey
Who have we become?

We all have one --
That particular instant of reflection
We question our essence
And our passage through life
It's as if all else stands still
Seize your moment

A Child's Dream

Just last night, a child had a dream
Of a place not far away
Where all are treated equally
No sadness touches the day

It is void of sorrow and pain
All signs of war have ended
People are showered with blessings
All fences have been mended

Just last night, a child had a dream
Of a place not far away
Where hatred is unknown
And love is the great mainstay

Where all races stand side by side
All hands are joined together
No fear or anguish is present
Hearts are light as a feather

Just last night, a child had a dream
Of a place not far away
Where affection warms our souls
Like the warmth of the sun's rays

A place where people are truly free
And everybody cares
It's a dream the children see clearly
A dream we all should share

SIMPLE TREASURES

Kisses
HONOR
SMILES
FAITH
Love
TRUTH
HUGS

Age 6

54

Chapter 4

Simple Treasures

We are all changed in some way by our experiences in life. I am forever changed by the events that have taken place in my life.

I could have chosen to concentrate on all the negative: the pain, the suffering, the lost time, the hysterectomy. In fact, without realizing it, I did just that for many months. I couldn't see past the gray of my afflictions.

Why did this happen to me? I don't have the answer to that question. I do know that because of what happened, I am stronger. I can now see past my suffering to the brilliant rainbow of color that lies ahead.

I awake each morning and thank God for one more day. I look at my beautiful children and I am filled with joy and pride. I think of my husband, my partner in this dance called life, and I smile. His love and devotion was and is incredible.

The little things in life have taken on new meaning for me. Or quite possibly, I have just learned to appreciate them.

I do believe our greatest treasures on earth are the simple things we take for granted. Our greatest treasures are the little things we blindly trample over in our race for something more.

The Little Things

Give thanks for the little things:
    a moment of quiet,
    a hug, a kiss,
    a smile shared,
    a stranger who cared.

Give thanks for the little things:
    to be able to laugh,
    a note from a friend,
    the morning sun,
    old fashioned fun.

Give thanks for the little things:
    truth and honor,
    fresh cookies from the oven,
    a car that will start,
    a gift from the heart.

Give thanks for the little things:
    umbrellas and raincoats,
    unconditional love,
    words unspoken,
    promises not broken.

Dare To Be

Don't be afraid to

Aim high.

Remember there is no

End

To what you can achieve.

Obey your heart and

Be strong.

Enthusiasm goes a long way!

58

Friends

Forever together

Ready to tackle the

Intricacies of life --

Everlasting bonds that can

Not be divided --

Definite

Strength in unity

A Seed Called Friendship

Once upon a time
Two souls planted a seed,
A seed called friendship --
They nurtured it
With salt from their tears
Warmth from their hearts
And covered it with pride
When storms threatened
With growth came metamorphosis --
It represented
Their similarities and differences
And in brilliant color
It represented their unity
Friendship prospered for years
Until the planters passed on,
No longer there
To nurture their friendship --
Just as a caterpillar
Becomes a butterfly
So did their friendship
Become a memory
And it continues to live,
As it flies with the beauty
Of the butterfly

Love

Love is special
It is unique to us all
Love gives you strength
To rise again when you fall
Love is swallowing your pride
Although you "know" you are right
Love apologizes first
When you have been in a fight
Love is sickening at times
Down-right no fun
Love is looking past the clouds
To see the sun
Love is a gift
Real from the start
Love is what I feel for you
Deep in my heart

We All Want To Be

We all want to be
Cheerful, polite, and honest
Hard working and well-liked
Popular and good-looking
Devoted and loyal
Always on time
Fun to be around
Nice, creative, and smart
With personality plus
Genuine and funny
Sincere and sympathetic

We all want to be
Simply fascinating
Friendly and energetic
The first to be invited
The last to be ignored
The epitome of friend
Wonderful, terrific, and happy
Strong and self-reliant
Never bored or sad
Confident and brave
Beautiful inside and out

....and able to leap tall obstacles
                    in a single bound!

This Is To Love You

To hear your words of concern and caring
Brings me peace of heart,
Seeing your special smile
When my world is falling apart

To laugh when I feel like crying
Just because you're near,
To hug you oh so tightly
When I am full of fear

To feel all the tears
Escaping my eye,
To feel your loving hand
Wiping them dry

You mean more to me
Than I could ever say.
I thank God for you
Each and every day.

To You: Michelle Lundell

I'll Stay By You

I'll stay by you
When the road gets rough
When you're all confused
No longer tough
When the wind blows cold ...
When the cards you've been dealt
Make you want to fold

I'll stay by you
When the others go
I'll bring you up
When you're feeling low --
Through both frowns and smiles
Together, you and I
Will cross the miles

I'll stay by you
When you're in need
In your heart's garden
I'll nurture each seed
I'll be there from now until the end
When you need a good cry
My shoulder, I'll lend

Inner Beauty

Beauty has many definitions
As it is seen through countless eyes
It may be the gorgeous toys one buys
Or the expensive items in the store
Beauty should be on the inside, at the very core

It may be the diamond rings one wears
Or the 14K gold dancing bears
Beauty at face value is not always true
One sees beauty, yet hasn't a clue
One keeps on searching, looking for the glitter
This endless search will make one bitter
Beauty surrounds us in everyday living
Sometimes as simple as selfless giving
The best kind of beauty comes from within
To deny this real beauty is simply a sin

If Only For A Moment

Think before you speak.

Keep a New Year's resolution.

Say no.

Try something new.

Use the exercise tape you bought last year.

Hug a child.

Say you are sorry first.

Smile more.

Worry less.

Thank your dad for being so strict.

Pray.

Be honest.

Listen.

Learn how to change a flat tire .. before you get one.

Love your enemy.

Put your true weight on your driver's license.

Follow a hunch.

Balance your checkbook.

Question things.

Believe in the unbelievable.

Let your actions speak louder than your words.

Keep a promise.

Call your mom.

Wish upon a star.

Break a rule.

Do the unexpected.

Forgive. Forgive. Forgive. Forgive.

Cherish a memory.

Love, and be loved.

Make something ordinary ... extra-ordinary.

Make a fantasy become a reality.

Laugh easily and often.

Remain calm amidst turmoil.

Be true to yourself.

Give honest compliments.

Learn from your mistakes.

In the hustle and bustle of everyday living ... there is a moment!

Chapter 5

In Loving Memory

"When you realized you were dying, were you afraid?"

This is a question I am asked often. In all honesty, I was not at all fearful of death. I was fearful of the pain because it was so intense. I was fearful that the burning, tugging, piercing pain would never go away. I feared that the process of dying would be very long and drawn out, but I did not fear death itself.

There was a moment during the terrible ordeal when I did feel a sense of peace. The voices in the room began to fade, and although I believe my eyes were open, I could not see anything. There was no color, no noise, no people, no pain. It was as if my heavily laden body had become light and I was floating inside myself.

Soon a nurse began saying my name, "Carissa ... Carissa, you have to be strong. Your baby needs you." I was suddenly reminded that I had just had a baby. Instantly, I was back in my world of pain and commotion.

I wasn't needed in heaven as much as I was needed on earth. My children needed their mommy.

I know there is a heaven. I have always believed that. When I faced possible death, I did not fear where I would go if I passed on. I knew the angels would show me the way. And those who had gone before me would be waiting -- arms open wide.

Passage Of Time

I can not tell you that your emotional chaos
Will suddenly transform into serene feelings,
That time will heal all wounds
Or that you will forget the tremendous pain --
However, time will ease the pain
And it won't hurt so much to remember
Don't let go of the memories
Don't push yourself to forget
Memories allow for continuance
Of the life that has passed on

Grandpa Harold

H   is for having a heart of gold

A   is for arms round his grandchildren fold

R   is for rather quiet and shy

O   is for original, one of a kind guy

L   is for lover of the outdoors

D   is for dearly loved evermore

71

Morris Parker Hall

I haven't forgotten you, Grandpa
I know I never will
A vacant spot remains in my heart
That only you can fill

Random memories fade with time
Vividly others remain
You felt a loss of youthful freedom
Relying on wheelchair and cane

"Are you my girl today?" you'd ask
While I'd giggle with delight.
"Only if you can catch me," I'd say
And I'd fly like a wind-blown kite.

Realizing you couldn't chase me
I'd inch closer to your chair
You would hook me with your cane
We were quite the pair

You would ask me to clean your glasses
I'd give them my best spit-shine
I'd ask, "How do they look, Grandpa?"
You'd answer, "Mighty fine!"

I recollect your favorite chair
Hee-Haw on T.V.
Copenhagen hidden in your pocket
Where Grandma couldn't see

You were the finest grandpa
Your memory is etched in my heart
One day we'll join hands in heaven
No longer far apart

Dennis Victor Ulrich

I wish I could have met you
Todd talks of you so much
Everyone misses you greatly
Just knowing you, they were touched

I wish I could have known you
Although I feel that I do
Because being close to Todd
Means being close to you

I hope that you can see us today
Your son and I, side by side
He's made me the happiest woman on earth
By taking me as his bride

I know you would be proud of your sons
And the wife you left behind
For your memory will live forever
In their hearts and in their minds

Even though you can not be here today
You are not far away
For the candles burn in your honor
And we remember you as we pray

The love we, as Christians, share
Is going to last forever
And in the very end
We ALL will be together

Werner Ulrich

W is for wonderful husband and friend

E is for everlasting love, without end

R if for real, one-of-a kind brother

N is for natural, devoted father

E is for embracing the grandchildren you love

R is for rare gift from above

U is for understanding, daring to care

L is for loyal, beyond compare

R is for respectable, in the way that you live

I is for invaluable advice that you give

C is for carefree, your fun-loving ways

H is for heavenly ... then and always

Donnie's Wings

Fond memories linger
Donnie's speedboat ... what fun!
Were there any boats faster?
To us, there were none

Your love for hunting
We fondly recall
The annual mens' trip up north
Was always a ball

You were lucky in love
When you found Mardell
And you were lucky a few times
In Vegas, as well

A better family man
Could not be found
You were a good listener
And your advice was sound

Nicknames were plentiful
Don Juan and Two-Shot
And of course, Uncle Donnie
To a handful of tots

We remember our Uncle Donnie
We reminisce to keep you near
Our memories of the good ole' days
Flash before us, ever clear

Your children miss you greatly
Lonely is your wife
There is one consolation
In heaven is true life

Through the memories in our hearts
Your presence round us sings
We think of you in heaven
As we know you've earned your wings

I initially began writing this book as a means of healing and as a tribute to my family and friends for their support. I hope <u>Fly Not Yet, My Princess</u> helped you, too, by broadening your smile and warming your heart.

<u>The Dance</u>, a song written by Tony Arata and sung by Garth Brooks, says it best …. "I could have missed the pain, but I'd of had to miss the dance."

Thanks for reading!

Index

Chapter 5 - In Loving Memory